IN THE NAME OF GOD

Entrepreneurship as done by

Engineer Peyman Kianian

The Founder of

Nafis Holding

Written by:
Dr. Reza Yadegari
Dr.Mahshid Sanaeefard
The Winners of the Prestigious
Jalal Al-e Ahmad Literary Award
and
Aryaan Yadegari
Lilyaan Yadegari
The Second Generation Authors of the
Great Iranian Entrepreneur Book Collection

Kidsocado Publishing House
Vancouver, Canada

Phone: +1 (833) 633 8654
WhatsApp: +1 (236) 333 7248
Email: info@kidsocado.com
https://kidsocadopublishinghouse.com
https:/kidsocado.com

Serial Number: P 2446190213

Title: Entrepreneurship as done by Engineer Peyman Kianian

Sub Title: The Founder of The Founder of Nafis Holding

Series Name: Iranian Great Entrepreneurs

Authors: Dr. Reza Yadegari, Dr. Mahshid Sanaeefard

Contributor Authors: Aryaan Yadegari, Lilyaan Yadegari

Copyist: Great Entrepreneur

ISBN: 978-1-77892-189-6

Metadata: Entrepreneurship/ Biography /Business & Economics

Book: Paperback

Pages: 84

Canada Publish Date: July 2024

Publisher: Kidsocado Publishing House

Introduction

The work of identifying the greatest Iranian entrepreneurs got underway back in 1997 with the help and assistance of my wife Dr. Mahshid Sanaeefard, the Manager of the Great Iranian Entrepreneurs Publication. An exceptionally long and arduous task, which has enabled us to gain substantial insight into the world of entrepreneurship and job creation, and thus make history for the future generation of Iranians by helping found and chart a whole new path towards true success in business and industry alike.

Next to winning numerous international awards on this incredible journey of countless ups and downs, we have cooperated and collaborated extensively with some of Iran's highly accredited and most reputable higher learning centers, like Sharif Industrial University, University of Science and Technology, Alzahra University and Shahid Beheshti University. Moreover, we have also successfully established and registered the International Qualification and Certification Auditors Company or IQCA in Canada, whose main role and responsibility is to publish the life history of the greatest Iranian entrepreneurs to make them known by name to the other people in the world. IQCA has

also been highly active in setting up and establishing an award presentation scheme in Iran in order to identify and introduce the country's most creative individuals and organizations, and thereby aid and assist with promoting them on a global scale.
It is hoped that as a special and leading group, we are able to introduce the most powerful Iranian women and me to the rest of the world and at the same time, identify and retell the life stories of the best role models for Iran's next generation.

Dr. Reza Yadegari
www.UNESCO.ws

The Greenlight

The movement to transfer the experiences of the world's greatest entrepreneurs is one of the most important factors in helping the American and European companies and organizations' progress and improvement. These companies and organizations had concluded rather smartly that if a society wishes significant advancement and development, it must keep its eye on the experiences of the previous generation and not allow the young to incur costs on the system by experiencing and learning through trial and error. In line with the same notion, entrepreneurship has the potential to create notable transformation throughout a given society's various levels provided it is implemented using principles and plans that take advantage of the experiences of the proficient and skilled members. Allowing the young to take over across the world is certainly a commendable measure, which has also been taken in our beloved Iran as well, except that here the experiences of the previous generation of entrepreneurs and managers has never been made properly available for application by the new generation – something that has regrettably inflicted irrecoverable costs onto the country because of the continuous repetition of the same old mistakes. Our project to identify the greatest Iranian entrepreneurs, so that we may research their lives to understand the reasons and factors for their success started off back in 1997 simultaneously as the arrival of the novel science of entrepreneurship in Iran. Admittedly, the path has been a long one involving strenuous effort. In the years following the events of the Iranian Revolution, literary no entrepreneur in the country was willing to unveil and reveal herself or himself and the experiences she or he possessed.

In spite of this, we were quite determined to fulfil our goal of teaching and training the future generation by documenting and publishing the life stories and experiences of Iran's greatest entrepreneurs through a one-thousand-volume book aptly titled 'Entrepreneurship as done by …' What is presented in the book collection, is rare and valuable roadmap designed based on the experiences and performances of Iran's greatest economic minds, which undoubtedly can be a wonderful asset in guiding and directing anyone who intends to get involved in any type of commercial, production and service provision activity. We hope that our collection book can help open up doors and pave the way for Iran's new generation of young entrepreneurs, and also remain a lasting piece of literary work to remember us by.

Dr. Reza Yadegari
Dr. Mahshid Sanaeefard
Tehran, Iran 2021

The life and world of

Peyman Kianian

Peyman Kianian

It seems like it was just yesterday when I walked out of school, in my final year of high school. That year, Kermanshah experienced heavy snowfall, and the weather was bitterly cold. You had to tread carefully to avoid slipping and falling, which would have been quite a misfortune at the end of the school year. I pulled my hat down over my ears and stepped out of the school building. I don't recall the exact day—it might have been late in the year, or perhaps it was my birthday, the 22nd of Esfand. When the bell rang, our teacher said the final sentence: "Don't forget that this year is a crucial one for you; this year, you'll rcap the rewards of all your hard work. From now on, everything is up to you." A few students in the back of the class started whispering. I don't know what was exchanged between them, but they all burst into laughter. Mr. Nazem Pour, our physics teacher, glared at them. He wouldn't have minded throwing his usual insult, "idiots," at us in his distinct accent. He muttered something under his breath, shook his head, and was preparing himself when the bell rang loudly. He raised his thick eyebrows, shrugged his shoulders, and said in the local dialect, "You know what to do."

My mind was preoccupied with Mr. Nazem Pour's words that day; I needed to think and plan. With all the thoughts swirling in my head, I felt like I could walk around the entire city. I don't know why that day felt different. My mind was filled with various scenes: my father, my mother, my family, and the role I had to play to repay even a fraction of my mother's efforts.

I had lost my father years ago when I was in the first year of middle school. My mother was my father's second wife. He had four sons and two daughters from his first marriage, and there were three of us: me, my sister, and my brother. My father worked for the regional electricity department. We weren't wealthy, but we were a kind and loving family. When my father was alive, our small house was always warm. Despite our financial struggles, my mother managed things well. She was always busy with something: knitting, sewing, taking care of household affairs, ensuring things didn't get too tough.

She used to tell me that when I was born, even though my father already had four sons and two daughters from his first marriage, he was overjoyed. From my childhood, the only things I remember are the green fields, beautiful nature, the crisp, fresh air, and the delightful aroma of the food my mother cooked. I also recall the mischief and games we played in the alley, kicking the ball with all our might and laughing so hard that our voices reached the sky. Our winters were marked by the smell of the kerosene heater struggling to warm our home, always losing five to nothing to the winter cold.

Back then, the only furniture in our house was an old, worn-out wardrobe in the corner of the living room, where my mother stored our few belongings. She had pasted our "Hundred Bravo" and "Thousand Bravo" cards from school on it.

When I reached school age, one early morning, my mother excitedly called me, "Peyman, get up!" The night before, she had explained that we needed to go to school for registration. Without a word, I got up, washed my face and hands, not fully understanding what school was about. I thought we were going there to play. After breakfast, we headed to the school, which wasn't far. They asked for my name and took a few photos. Just like that, I embarked on a path I grew to love more each day. On the way back, my mother advised me to study hard, saying, "Son, an uneducated person is blind. Study hard and make something of yourself." This advice continued until I entered university. These were not just empty words or gentle persuasion; sometimes they came with a mix of force and scolding. Back then, parents didn't believe much in talking; they conveyed their intentions more through actions. As they say, their intentions were good, but their way of expressing them was not!

Days went by, and I finished elementary school and moved on to middle school. I remember when my father left us forever and passed away. I was in my first year of middle school. At the funeral, everyone who passed by offered condolences, patted me on the head, and said, "From now on, you are the man of the house."

From that moment, the heavy burden of being the man of the house fell on my shoulders. I felt a greater sense of responsibility. After my father's death, it felt as if I grew up in just one week. I matured quickly, studied more, played less, and took better care of my sister and brother. Additionally, I had to look after my mother, who now slept even less, staying up late to sew and add to the meager pension income. I did my best, but whenever I worried about her, she would kindly say, "My dear, focus on your studies; that's more important." So, I studied hard, sitting beside my mother, who stayed up late sewing clothes for neighbors. After dinner, when we laid out the bedding and went to sleep, my mother's work would begin. We had an old transistor radio that she placed on the shelf. She would take it down, set it beside her on the floor, turn it on, and start working. The steady clatter of the sewing machine, combined with the soft sound of the radio, would carry my thoughts far away. I would place my hands under my head and stare into space. Often, I would just stare, but sometimes my thoughts would take flight, usually imagining that I had become very wealthy and would no longer allow my mother to work so hard. Then, feeling tired and not wanting to think anymore, I would turn over, pull the blanket over my head, close my eyes, and not realize when I fell asleep.

I recalled that day when I came home from school, put my books aside, and changed my clothes. Mother had made lentil rice for lunch. After eating, I got busy with my homework. We had planned to play soccer with the kids in the afternoon. My eyes were on the book, but my attention was more on the doorbell. I had already done my homework and was pretending to be busy with my books so that my mother wouldn't ask me to do anything, especially not send me out to buy bread. My mother was busy working, talking, and taking care of my little sister. I was wondering why Gholam hadn't arrived yet; he should have shown up by now. As if reading my mind, my mother, still busy, asked, "Are you going to play soccer with Gholam again?" I buried my head deeper into the book and pretended not to hear. I had nothing to say. It had been a while since my mother had been doing all the household chores by herself. I thought to myself, it's the kids' fault for not leaving me alone, saying it wouldn't be the same without me. I played as a forward and scored most of the goals, so the kids always came looking for me. I was really on a roll with my game. I pouted and glanced at my mother but didn't dare to confirm her words.

When the doorbell rang, I quickly gathered my books and notebooks and put them aside. Mother didn't even look at me or raise her head, but her expression clearly showed she was upset. My younger brother and sister sensed that things weren't quite right and quietly watched us. For a moment, I hesitated to leave. When I went to open the door, I noticed it was cold and cloudy, perhaps it was going to rain. I could use that as an excuse not to go. As I opened the door, Gholam rushed into the yard and hurriedly said, "Why haven't you put on your shoes yet?" I replied,

"The weather isn't good. I don't feel like playing in the rain." He said, "It's more fun in the rain. Haven't you seen the foreign football matches?" I said, "They play on grass, not in the dirt of an alley." He insisted that the kids were waiting and that it wouldn't be the same without me. I said, "Just one game," and he agreed. I left Gholam at the door and went back to put on my sneakers. For a moment, my eyes met my mother's; she gave me a sideways glance but said nothing. I felt that I would have to pay for this decision later, but the urge to play was stronger. Plus, what could I do with Gholam eagerly waiting at the door? I feared he might go back and say something to the other kids that would embarrass me.

I put on my sneakers and went to the door. Gholam grabbed my hand and pulled me towards the alley, closing the door behind us. I said, "Just one game, and if it starts raining heavily, I'm coming back home." Gholam eagerly replied, "Okay, okay, let's go."

Our soccer field was the next street over, which was a bit wider, and the neighbors didn't mind. As I turned the corner, I saw the kids waiting, having already set up the goalposts with bricks. Without a word, I picked up the plastic ball that lay in the middle of the street and started playing.

While playing, I glanced at Mr. Asadollahi's bakery. There was no one in line; it was completely empty. I thought to myself, what luck! If I had come to buy bread, there would have been twenty people in line. I decided that after this game, I'd go get the bread and head straight home.

But I kept playing. The bakery started to get crowded. I thought, just one more game and a goal... Meanwhile, I kept thinking about the bakery, which now had a significant line of customers. Gradually, I got really into the game, and before I knew it, I had stayed for all the games, most of the kids had gone home, and it was getting dark. I shook myself and started towards home, fear and anxiety about my mother's scolding filling me. The closer I got to home, the faster my heart beat. I knocked, and my little brother opened the door, not even looking at me before walking away. I quietly entered the house and slipped into the bathroom to wash my hands and feet. Why was the house so quiet? Why wasn't anyone making any noise? After leaving the bathroom, I sat next to the closet, wanting to hide in the gap between the closet and the wall. Mother peeked out of the kitchen but said nothing. She was busy preparing dinner. She turned to my brother and said, "If you're hungry, set the table." Setting the table was usually my job, but she didn't ask me that night. She then stirred the last spoonful in the pot, placed the lid on it, and took out the dishes from the shelf. I didn't know what to do. Aimlessly, I got up and went to the small room where the bedding was stored. My eyes fell on the shopping bag still sitting in the corner of the room, which she hadn't had time to put away. She had told me several times to buy laundry detergent because we had run out, but I had ignored her. Now she had gone and bought it herself, probably standing in line for a long time since detergents were rationed back then. I was dying of regret. I promised myself that from now on, I would listen to whatever she said. I prayed for her to talk to me and vowed not to cause her any trouble from now on. But even at the dinner table, we were all silent. Mother served dinner to everyone and called the kids, but she didn't pay any attention to me. I sat at the table, but I couldn't swallow my food, despite having played so much and being very hungry. The food stuck in my throat and went down slowly, bit by bit. I barely ate and escaped to the yard. Usually, during these times, Mother would ask why I didn't finish my food or why I ate so little. I was waiting for her to say something, but she didn't. I went and sat on the veranda, feeling like crying. I thought about the goals I had scored, the cheers of the kids, and how engrossed I had been in the game. I imagined Gholam and the other kids sitting around their dinner tables, talking with their parents, watching TV, and laughing, while I sat here feeling miserable. I was on the verge of tears. I couldn't take it anymore; I got up and went to the room where she was taking the dishes to the kitchen. With a choked voice, I said, "I'm sorry, I'm sorry, I swear I won't go without permission again. I swear I'll listen to whatever you say. Mom, please forgive me." She put the dishes down, placed her hand on my head, and said, "My dear..." That night, I realized how much I depended on my family, and I never again prioritized my own desires over her wishes.

I remembered the day I arrived late to school. The kids were already in class, and our principal was standing in the hallway, shouting, "Shut the door 1/2! Why are you making so much noise 2/3?" When he saw me, he frowned and said, "Why are you late, Kianian? Hurry to your class, the bell has rung." I hurried down the hallway to my class. As I passed the office, I peeked in to see if our first-period teacher had arrived. I only saw one or two teachers from the group. I couldn't stop and stare. Before I entered the classroom, our class monitor, Aryan, saw me and mischievously said, "Quiet, guys! The teacher is here!" The class fell silent. Just as I was about to enter, Aryan shouted, "Stand up!" The kids stood up, and as soon as they saw me, the class erupted in laughter, and a barrage of pens and paper airplanes flew my way.

I remembered our adolescence during the war, as if it were just yesterday. The moment the red alert siren sounded, the power would go out. If the Iraqi planes had come a few minutes later, I could have finished reading the last few pages. But most of the time, the power went out just a few pages before the end of the lesson.

During those times, we would go to the rooftop with the neighborhood kids to "track" the Iraqi planes, as we called it, boasting about our knowledge of planes and recounting what we had seen with our own eyes—how the anti-aircraft guns fired and made the planes flee. I remembered the night my mother, worried, forbade me from going to the rooftop anymore. She called me and said, "Come sit with me, it's the best place." I went and sat next to her. She kindly said, "If you're not here, and a thief comes in this darkness, what would we do without you?" Seeing how much my mother relied on me made me very happy, and I felt that in my father's absence, I was the man of the house and needed to stay home. Despite everything, I finally finished the third year of middle school. At the end of the year, I managed to pass with a bit of a leap. When I received my report card, I finally understood the joy of studying. Although my grades were good before, they had noticeably improved.

High school was a different world—newer, larger. We were almost all kids from the same neighborhood who had come from middle school together, full of ideas and dreams, experiencing both the mischief of childhood and the maturity of adulthood. Six days a week, I woke up early at 6 AM and went to school. On the way, I met another classmate who was a friend, and we walked to school together. He always had something to talk about, and we laughed at his silly stories as we made our way to school.

As we entered the school gates, a large courtyard greeted us, its walls covered with slogans and moral sayings. "Seek knowledge even if it is in Mars," "Knowledge is a treasure that never depletes," "If your tree bears the fruit of knowledge, you will conquer the celestial wheel," "Seek knowledge from the cradle to the grave," "No ease comes without effort," and "Spending time in teaching is better than striving in God's path." We saw these slogans every day and repeated them in our minds. Soon after, we lined up for the morning assembly and listened, somewhat reluctantly, to the principal's speeches and advice before heading to our classes.

The good thing was that on snowy and cold winter days, we were exempt from this duty. Thinking back, I laugh at how much we dreaded lining up. We passed through the corridors, with semi-organized rows, past the wall newspapers and bulletin boards, and entered our classrooms. If we strayed from the line, the principal would shout, “Don’t mess up the line!” and we’d shuffle back into place. But once we reached the classroom door, no one could stop us from shoving our way inside. Then it was just us and the classes—chemical equations, English grammar, physics, and other subjects. Back then, everyone dreamed of becoming doctors, engineers, or pilots. But I had something else in mind. I wanted a job to help support my family. Watching my mother work so hard to provide the basic necessities for a family of four wasn’t easy. Of course, we tried to help as much as we could with part-time jobs, summer work, and after-school jobs. But that wasn’t what I wanted. I wanted to make a real difference.

Life has its own path, and whether you like it or not, time passes with all its hardships and ups and downs. Time moved on for us too, and I reached the day when I walked through the city, my hat pulled down to my ears, hands frozen, head full of ideas and thoughts, not knowing where to unload the burden. That day, I realized that thoughts have weight. Even though they are in your head, they can weigh down your shoulders.

The year of the college entrance exam can be the best and worst year of your life. It paints a hazy picture of the future. From the moment we entered the fourth year of high school, every teacher who came to class would start by reminding us that we had the college entrance exam that year and needed to do certain things.

Each had their own set of instructions, recommendations, and encouragements based on their own success, urging us to study hard and review our lessons. One of our teachers was always scolding us, calling us fools and telling us to study because it was our final year and we didn't have much time left, ultimately concluding that we would all end up as laborers. Another teacher advised us that we were the future of the country and needed to study to build our nation.

On that cold day, I don't know why Mr. Khalatbari was kind. There were only a few days left until the New Year. He was supposed to test us. He entered the classroom, went to the desk, slowly placed his bag on it, pulled back his chair, looked at it, and sat down. He glanced at his watch, opened the grade book, then looked up and asked, "We were supposed to have a test today, right?" I was always ready to answer and had no problem, but as usual, the whole class raised their voices, saying, "No, sir, we didn't study. Sir, please don't test us this session..."

He got up angrily from behind his desk, went to the blackboard, picked up a piece of chalk, and wrote an incomprehensible word with force. Then he threw the chalk and pursed his lips. We were ready for his famous rebuke, but he quickly regained his composure and started walking between the desks. He asked, "Who were the top three students last year?" I and two others raised our hands. He asked, "How many of you passed with compensatory courses?" A few raised their hands. He said, "So, have you become good students this year or not?" The whole class laughed. He gave us a disappointed and worried look and continued, "Study your lessons well. I want all of you to succeed." He paused for a few moments, "I want to see all of you in your rightful places. You must repay your debt to this country. Besides thinking about yourselves, your families, and your city, you must think about the future of this country. Each of you will eventually become a father, so think about that. Just as each of you might become a doctor, a teacher, a shopkeeper, or a farmer, or even a shepherd, no matter how small your job is, you will have an impact on society. Your work affects your children and others. Even if you become a shopkeeper and are not careful about the products you sell, giving a child expired milk or chocolate, you create a chain of harm that repeats in society. You must strive to improve yourselves and do your work with conscience and in the best possible way."

He spoke, and I listened. His words had a profound impact on me. My head was throbbing. I felt as if a strong electric current was running through my body. I had never looked at the subject from this perspective. I just wanted to study to get a good job and help my family. Now, our teacher had opened my eyes to a much larger view. My motivation increased manifold. I had always been a good student, and that cold day, my motivation grew even more. When I came to my senses, I had walked half the city in the cold, my head buried in my shoulders, my face and nose frozen. Of course, the city wasn't very large at that time; a mix of mud and brick houses and new brick houses with sloping roofs, with no tall buildings. The only two-story building with a stone facade was the central National Bank building.

Our house was at the Silos intersection, on the eastern edge of the city. A bit further up was Fermanfarma Street, which had been widened in 1980 and renamed Seyyed Jamal al-Din Street. At the end of the street was Shahnaz Square. On the southeast corner of the Silos intersection was the new and modern building of the Kermanshah Tobacco Company, which is still there, and across from it, at the Silos boundary, was the Grain and Sugar Administration. With these thoughts and memories, I had walked the whole way in the freezing cold without realizing it. At least I had decided to stop thinking about working and focus on the entrance exam.

Autumn passed, winter passed, and spring came. The earth turned green, the snow receded to the peaks, rivers swelled and roared, trees budded and blossomed. The day I took my last exam and returned home, I was happy and joyful. I put my books in the closet and said, “It’s over! School is over!” When the New Year ended, all extracurricular activities were also over. I just studied. That year was one of the most beautiful years of my life, full of hope and motivation, a year full of ideas, staying up late, and making all kinds of plans.

The entrance exam was held in mid-July. The midday summer sun was scorching my brain. I was shifting my books in my sweaty hands and praying to be accepted.

Almost everyone knew when the newspapers would arrive, but I had developed an unusual obsession with going to the newsstand every morning to check the newspapers and ask the owner about them. Initially, he would respond with impatience: “I don't know. We'll put them out front whenever they arrive. Next month, next week, a few days..."

One day, he responded with dissatisfaction, "Do you have to come and ask every day?" I replied, "I can't help it; I'm stressed." He laughed and asked, "Would you like some tea?" I nodded. He said, "Whatever is meant to happen will happen; leave it to God." I said, "Yes! But I want to know the results as soon as possible." Gradually, my excitement spread to him, and every time he saw me, he would laugh and say, "It's almost time." We would chat for a bit, and then I would leave. On the day the results were due, the front of the newsstand was crowded with future students like me. I went up and greeted him. He laughed and came out of the stand, putting his hand on my shoulder and saying, "God willing, you'll pass. Don't worry." Although I was a good student, I still felt anxious. Back then, the number of participants was very high, and passing the entrance exam was a major and challenging task.

Finally, the waiting ended, and the newspapers arrived. The first newspaper was handed to me. I had to find my name, Kianian. Peyman Kianian... Kiani... Kianipour... Kianzad... Arashia Kianian... Babak Kianian... Bahram... Pouria... Peyman Kianian. I checked my father's name and checked again and again. It was me. It was really me.

My eyes were dry. I can confidently say that the feeling I experienced at that moment was incomparable to any other, and I have never felt such excitement, anxiety, and happiness elsewhere. It was the most beautiful moment of my life. I barely swallowed and lowered the newspaper, not trusting my eyes. I told myself to stay calm. After a few seconds, I raised the newspaper to my eyes again and read. I had seen correctly; Peyman Kianian! I had been accepted to Sharif University. I didn't know whether to walk or fly the distance from the newsstand to home. When I opened the door, my mother was sitting in the yard, waiting. Seeing my face, she came towards me and hugged me. There was no need to say anything. She hugged me and showered me with affection, constantly saying, "Congratulations, my dear! Congratulations to us, my dear."

I was bursting with joy. I wanted to tell the whole city that I had been accepted to Sharif University. I wanted to tell everyone I saw on the street that I had been accepted to university. You have to be from the 50s to understand how difficult it was to get accepted to university with such a large number of participants, and how crucial it was for us, who were like sandbags, to achieve this. Shortly after, I realized I had also been accepted as a scholarship student at Abbaspoor University. What could be better than this? For me, who was looking for income while studying, getting a scholarship was certainly the best possible situation.

I was lost in these thoughts and floating on clouds. It would take some time before I would go and register at the university. I had to think about whether to choose Abbaspoor or Sharif. This choice didn't take long. In the meantime, two events occurred that completely changed the path of my life. First, due to the usual and prevalent strictness of the time, which had no proper basis, I failed the Abbaspoor interview. My various and logical and childish reasons, trying to escape that predicament, were futile. My talent and ability were overlooked, and with a few ideological questions that might have been the interviewer's personal interpretation, they decided to reject me. I was left with Sharif. It was still very good. It was still excellent. But another event was about to happen.

It was evening. As usual, I had gone to buy bread. When I returned, I noticed we had a guest. A pair of large black men's shoes were neatly placed in front of the room. I heard talking. When I looked through the window, I saw that my uncle was there, talking, and my mother had her head down, saying nothing, just listening quietly and sadly, occasionally nodding in agreement. I felt as if her tears would fall at any moment. I coughed to make them aware of my presence and offered bread. He declined. Then he finished the last sip of his tea and said, "Sister, think about it." Then he got up, said goodbye, and left. My mother immediately cleared the tea set and went into the kitchen. I realized something was up. On the pretext of putting away the bread, which had dried in my hands, I followed her. I was looking for the breadbasket, but unlike usual, my mother wasn't paying attention at all. I asked, "Has something happened?" She didn't answer. I stood in front of her and asked again, "Mother, has something happened?" She said, "No, your uncle says we should build on our land. Now is a good time; materials are cheap, and the weather is warm. If Peyman goes to university, there won't be anyone to help you. On the other hand, the landlord, who was my mother's cousin, had temporarily given us part of his house, and we were supposed to move out once we built on our land. Our staying in his house was really causing him trouble." My legs gave way. It felt as if all the blood in my body rushed to my face. Why were the depths of our joys so shallow? Why hadn't I considered what my family would do if I left? I felt like such a bad son. I felt how badly I had failed in my duties and how crushing this feeling of self-blame was. I no longer knew what I wanted. I was bewildered. A heart that was broken, a resolve that was faltering. The thought of working crept back into my mind.

That night, I went to bed without dinner. My mother served food to the kids but didn't eat anything herself. I had never seen her show any sign of weakness or frown at the problems we faced, but that night, I clearly saw helplessness in her eyes. I wasn't sure if I wanted to continue, to leave and abandon my family—a family whose entire life was about wrestling with and fighting against adversity. But what about my own dreams and aspirations?

My face was burning, and I had a headache. I wanted to cry, but I pretended otherwise, attributing it to stupidity, exhaustion, the night, and my father's absence. I tried to comfort myself, rubbing my hands together, smiling, and motivating myself, telling myself that everything would get better. I kept telling myself, "Everything will be fine! You'll see, everything will be resolved! A miracle will happen, some money will come in, and we'll build our house, and I'll go on to pursue my studies at the university." But my eyes would fill with tears again. I kept repeating to myself that it was nothing, that it was just because I hadn't slept well, and that I should go and take a long shower right now. But nothing improved.

There are times in life when you want to run straight ahead and hang yourself. You feel so unhappy that you think you'll never get better, that no door will ever open for you. But after a while, you can lift your head and stand up again, hoping to catch a glimpse of some light, water, or greenery and feel the ground beneath your feet becoming firmer. It wasn't possible to walk in the depths of this despair. It wasn't in my capacity to ignore my family and pursue my own fortunes and life. One evening, near sunset, as I was wandering aimlessly, I stood by a wall, leaned against it, raised my head, and said, "God, help me make the right decision."

And I made a decision that was monumental for me at that time, a decision that felt like jumping off a cliff, like tearing oneself apart. I placed an advertisement to exchange my student placement, willing to go anywhere that offered the chemical engineering program for petroleum process design. A student was quickly found! Who wouldn't want to study at Sharif University? In this exchange, I received five million tomans and a spot at a university in a smaller city. This five million tomans and the university slot in a provincial area became the means to build a small house that could be a permanent shelter for my family. There was a bittersweet happiness in my heart. I was still unsure whether I had done the right thing or not. On my way back home, these doubts kept repeating in my mind. I foolishly spent time pondering them, and I don't know how or why, but one of my father's words came to mind: "Some people live, and some people die; the only thing that remains after death, the only thing that matters, the only thing that others remember, is the goodness of a person." I told myself that if one day I were to die, at least let my family have a better image of me in their memories.

So, I mentally closed the file on Sharif University and headed home with the good news. I loved my family and my mother, and this attachment made the hardships of this decision bearable for me. I knocked on the door and entered the yard, announcing happily, "It's done, we have the money to build the house." Everyone ran outside. My mother's face was full of tears, and I started crying too. Amidst sighs and tears, she kissed my face and thanked me. I felt a great sense of relief. When she kissed my face for the umpteenth time and stroked my hair, kissing it, there was not the slightest feeling of regret or sadness left in me. Our house was built, and as it neared completion, I left for university. It was the first year that Mazandaran University offered the process design program. Since I had been accepted to one of the best universities in the country, my academic level and knowledge were higher than that of other students. I quickly grasped the materials, and I didn't slack off in studying, researching, and reading there either.

It didn't take long for me to become known among the students and professors. From the second semester onward, familiar with the city and university, I started working as a student teacher, tutoring other students, and from the very beginning, I did not burden my family with any expenses. In fact, I started sending money and helping out. I lived very frugally, trying not to spend even the smallest amount to avoid extending my hand for help or needing to ask my mother for money. I didn't even travel back and forth. I would go home at the beginning of the term and visit them for a few days at the end of the term, always being warmly welcomed. My mother always complained about how infrequently I visited, and I never told her that I was saving even the little cost of bus fare. I lived through those four years, studying, flipping through newspapers, tidying my small dorm room, attending my classes, going straight and coming back, reading books, struggling, resisting, negotiating, compromising, shouting, denying, progressing, fighting, dealing, being happy, being sad, surrendering, resisting, moving forward, stepping back, stumbling, falling, getting up, arguing, giving up, and always being concerned about the future—my own, my mother's, and my younger siblings'. This concern never left me, although it would vary in intensity depending on the circumstances, but it never waned. Nor did my excitement for progress diminish. Many of my classmates had put all their energy into getting accepted, and once they were in, it was as if they had run out of fuel. They no longer showed much interest in studying and were content with just attending classes and lectures. But for me, the real story had just begun. I had just emerged from my shell, just left that familiar city and neighborhood, and was getting acquainted with different cultures and environments. I was working and learning new experiences every day, moving forward. The trust and attention I received from the professors, who clearly valued and supported me, boosted my confidence and motivated me even more.

In 1999, I graduated with top grades. I returned my dormitory key, moved to Tehran, and rented a small place. The job market in Tehran was better, and I planned to take the entrance exam for a master's degree. So, I needed a few days of rest. I visited my family for a few days. Spring had arrived, and the warm sun felt pleasant in the cool air. Looking at the mountains, you could still see the remnants of winter snow.

The plains had turned into meadows, with shades of green, yellow, purple, and many other colors! Especially after each rain, wildflowers would sprout from everywhere, even from between the rocks. The river was full of water, so cold that you couldn't keep your feet in it for more than a few minutes. I was happy. There was a sense of contentment under my skin. I was full of excitement, sometimes leaning my head against the wall and basking in the warmth of the sun. I would sit on the balcony, look down, and feel proud of the journey I had climbed. I would close my eyes and imagine myself leaping from boulders, ascending to a fortress where no one had ever been, then standing with my arms outstretched, letting my thoughts soar. Sometimes, I would see my father's smiling face. Then, I would be brought back to reality by my mother's voice, usually bringing something to eat, like tea or fruit. She would sit next to me, chatting about everything, and I would laugh, listening lightly to her words. I was content with myself, happy that she was pleased with me.

After some time, relaxing, it was time to return and prepare for the next round. The day I was leaving, my mother saw me off with a bowl of water and worried eyes. She was unhappy about my departure and insisted that I stay, start a family there, and find a job. But I had bigger plans for my life. As I was saying goodbye, I told her to set those thoughts aside and come visit me whenever she wanted. She said, "Alright, go! But you know I'm always worried about you." I laughed heartily, hugged her, and said, "Don't be." As soon as I got back home, I started studying again and, on another summer day, took the master's entrance exam and succeeded once more. I became the 11th rank in the Sharif University master's program—Peyman Kianian from Kermanshah.

Now, perhaps more than ever, I appreciated my achievements. Maybe now I could better use this success and manage it more effectively. I was no longer that young, inexperienced boy from a small town who had arrived in a big city. I knew how to work; I had learned to present myself and show my abilities to others. I had learned how to earn an honest living. I knew how to fend for myself and take care of my family.

These were all things I had worked hard for and valued greatly. This success had been painstakingly nurtured. I was happy that I had managed to win my mother's approval and achieve my dreams, even if it was a bit later and farther away. But now, I was wiser, more mature, and more thoughtful.

I resumed teaching. I taught both at an institute and privately. For a while, I also worked in the R&D department at Supa Company and participated in a joint project between Iran Khodro, Sapco, and the university to gain more work experience. I was earning well, so much so that I no longer worried about daily expenses and could even save a little. Near the end of my graduation, the idea of going abroad crossed my mind. Most of my peers agreed on this. Many of our professors taught not only at Sharif University but also at various universities in the United States, and their recommendations could expedite our departure. I was a well-known student, and my relationships with university professors were very good. If I requested a recommendation, it would be quickly accepted.

Therefore, after consulting, researching, and reviewing, I realized that I could easily get accepted abroad and pursue my PhD. I applied to the University of Texas and was overjoyed to be accepted. I wanted to go now that I felt at ease with my family's situation and start a new life. When the university's acceptance letter arrived, I went to my hometown and straight to our house to share the news with my mother first. I waited until evening when my siblings were also there and then excitedly started telling the story.

My childhood mischief hadn't entirely left me; we sat down happily at the table. I started joking and teasing my siblings. We were talking and laughing. But as soon as I mentioned that I wanted to go to America, my mother's eyes widened. "Where?

America?" she said with anger, "You're not going anywhere. I didn't sacrifice my youth for you all just for you to leave for the other side of the world when it's time for me to enjoy your presence."

I reasoned with her, laughed, talked about how our financial situation would improve, how I could help more, how I could bring her to live with me after a while, and how I could pave the way for my younger brother, Yazdan, who was also an engineering student at Razi University. I talked about the benefits there, the facilities, the healthcare, and social services... but she heard none of it. She quickly cleared the table, instructing my sister to pass this and take that away while I kept talking. Finally, she said, "You want to go? Go ahead, do whatever you want, but I'm no longer your mother. I won't forgive you, and I won't bless you with my milk!" And with that, she ended the conversation.

Of course, I have never regretted it. Not for not emigrating, nor for not securing a government job for myself. Nowhere in the world is like one's own country. When you first arrive abroad, everything seems glamorous—clean streets, vast commercial buildings, wide roads. But all these things lose their novelty after a while. As soon as you get used to it, homesickness hits, and you start longing for your homeland. Often, when I travel, I stand by the hotel room window for a long time, watching the streets and life passing by below. Watching the shadows of buildings grow longer as the sun moves west. I don't try to shape my thoughts in those moments. In this state, many things lose their abstract meaning and become more tangible.

The social welfare and tranquility of the people walking on the streets are certainly enticing. However, after some time, these things become ordinary, and that's when you start to miss everything back home.

In any case, in the year 2000, I got a part-time job at a trading company. Their business was importation, and their main products were citric acid and overhead cranes. I was hired with the minimum wage set by the Ministry of Labor, which was 120,000 tomans. Meanwhile, my peers were working in major industries like atomic energy, defense industries, the Ministry of Oil, or government-affiliated companies, making the most of the opportunities available to them. They had monthly salaries of one million tomans, mobile phones, company housing, and cars. However, due to the sensitivity and issues that led to my initial rejection at the university's local investigations, I couldn't find a job in any of these organizations. This could have been a source of disappointment for me, knowing that academically I was on par with my peers, yet I hadn't secured a fitting social and professional position in any organization or institution. But I wasn't actively pursuing it either. I enjoyed my work. During the interview, the company owner told me, "We have a lot of potential for work here. If you really want to get things done, you'll have both freedom and sufficient resources." I replied that I was interested in importing raw materials for cosmetics, hygiene products, and pharmaceuticals, and I believed it could be an attractive field that would bring many clients to the company. He said, "Start and give it a try."

When I checked the company's financial statements, I realized that the total revenue was less than a billion tomans, around one million dollars. I began writing letters, talking, networking, holding endless meetings, running around, and engaging in the exhausting game of finding clients and suppliers. I was entrenched, determined to seize the front lines. I had designed and planned everything based on a realistic map. I envisioned everything and enjoyed this vision. I loved working; simultaneously, I was studying, engaging in trade, and consulting companies on product formulation and improvement. It was good. Everything was going well. I had managed to turn my inexperience into a winning position.

I stayed at that company until 2004, for four years. I enjoyed being productive and felt satisfaction from significantly increasing the company's efficiency. By then, many well-known brands like Atosa and Alborz were sourcing their raw materials from us. We had obtained about ten official representations for raw material procurement, and the company's annual financial statements had reached ten billion tomans. All this effort resulted in 13 million tomans in savings, a significant amount at the time.

Finally, one summer morning, at precisely 7:20 AM, as I stood in front of the mirror to shave and get ready for work, I decided I wanted to work for myself. I told myself that I could no longer go to that company. That morning, for the first time since I started my professional career, I doubted my current path. Despite all the risks and uncertainties, I realized that I wanted to have my own business.

Of course, small, bothersome thoughts crept into my mind, like termites gnawing away. What if you can't do it? What if it doesn't work out? What if you lose this investment too? What if you fail? Can you really do it? And I looked at myself and my eyes in the mirror and said confidently, yes, you can, you definitely can. At that moment, there was nothing impossible for me.

Upon arriving at the company, I requested a meeting and, to everyone's surprise, I submitted my resignation to the chairman and CEO. He didn't take it seriously at first, and started talking, saying that I was like a son to him and that he didn't want me to leave the company under any circumstances. He asked why I wanted to leave. I told him that I thought I would be more successful working for myself at this stage. He asked if something had caused me dissatisfaction or if I didn't like my working conditions. He even said that if I wanted a raise, it was no problem, I just had to ask. I explained that it was none of those things. The only reason was that I thought it was better to work for myself. He asked if I wanted to be a shareholder. I smiled and didn't say anything, just nodded. He left the room with displeasure.

The next day, he called me in and said, "Engineer Kianian, I have a new plan. If you agree, we can start a new company where you own 50% and we own 50%. Think about it." I told him that I had already made up my mind and asked him to agree to let me go. I assured him that my decision had nothing to do with the benefits he mentioned. I wanted to work for myself and promised not to approach any of their clients or brands. Despite this, it took several months for him to give his consent. But in the end, he relented, and I parted ways with the group.

Interestingly, for a long time afterward, whenever we saw each other at various events or exhibitions, despite my approaching him, greeting him warmly, and kissing his hand out of respect, he would turn away and not respond to my greeting. I truly felt indebted to him. His company had been my launchpad. It wasn't until years later, when he was assured that I had kept my word and had not approached any of his clients or suppliers, that he reconciled with me.

During my time at that trading company, I had gained enough experience to know which materials had higher sales in the market and how to connect with those who demanded these goods. The company had given me the opportunity to learn about trading, to lead negotiations, meetings, and foreign trips to secure representations. Previously, I had obtained raw material representations for that company, so I couldn't completely move away from them. I spent some time researching and investigating. I had become an expert and knew where to look for things. However, the more I investigated, the less I achieved my desired results. I was getting frustrated, and I had no income, yet I didn't want to touch my savings at all. But it wasn't the time to surrender. I had taken big risks to get to this point. I had promised myself that I would make myself proud. To achieve success, I had to wear a suit of armor. At any cost, no failure was acceptable.

After a few months, a spark was ignited, and the comfort of relief washed over me like warm spring water. I finally found a Japanese company that supplied the raw material for hair gel, which increased its viscosity. I started corresponding and talking with them. They said their Middle Eastern sales were handled by a German company and that I should speak to their representative there.

The process of correspondence and discussions began. I got a price quote. When I tested the samples, I found that despite being able to procure it at a lower price, it also saved 20% of the raw material. This meant that by using 20% less Japanese carbomer, I could achieve the same desired viscosity as the previous gels, and this was excellent. I requested representation. Initially, they didn't agree to grant me the representation. I had to work with them for a while and purchase a specific amount. When I spoke with the representative, he said they were willing to have a sales representative in Iran, but it was unusual to make such a decision quickly. I needed to make a minimum purchase of 10 tons within a year. I thought for a moment. Having this representation would give me more independence and many benefits. So, I agreed and said, "I accept, but I have one condition. Have you ever received any requests or contacts from Iran?" He said no and assured me that for a year, any emails or calls from Iran would be referred to me for negotiation. With this, our negotiations were finalized, and I made my first purchase of

1 ton. It cost 9 million tomans, and the dollar was around 800 tomans at the time. The stock sold quickly, and with the profit I made, I purchased 2 tons. Business was going well, and I had good sales. After working with 2 batches, I was confident that I could sell and succeed.

However, waiting for the materials to arrive, sell them, and then buy again was neither logical nor economical. I needed to find funds. The first idea that came to mind was getting a loan. My bank account was with Bank Melli, Naderi branch. I went directly to the bank manager, laid out all my academic and company documents, and honestly explained the situation. I told him that all my financial transactions for these two batches had been done through this bank and would continue to be. But I truly had no other collateral or deposit. I desperately needed this money. The bank manager asked many questions, and at the end of the meeting, he shook my hand and said, "I can open a $2 million letter of credit for you." It was a significant step. Incredible. A $2 million loan. It was great, and that enabled me to import 110 tons of raw materials in the coming year instead of 10 tons. Since I also did consulting, formulation, and reformulation for other companies, selling the product didn't seem difficult, and the materials sold quickly upon arrival. This continued, and I made good investments. But continuing this way didn't seem logical either. So, I decided not to put all my eggs in one basket and invested in various places. I bought property in Dubai, a cattle farm with a hundred cows in Hashtgerd City, and did similar investments. Then, I decided to get into production myself and become a manufacturer. I thought of various products to produce, which eventually led me to hair care products. Gels, shampoos, and other hygiene products that had a good market.

But I had to market them differently. I wasn't yet able to buy a factory and start production here, which, in a way, was my winning card. During a business trip to France, I realized that registering a company there not only added credibility to the products but was also relatively easier compared to other countries. I liked the name Crystal. It was an international name, pleasant sounding, and had a positive connotation.

So, I registered the Crystal brand in France. I also registered it with the Chambers of Commerce in Iran. Then I negotiated with a manufacturing plant in Strasbourg to produce the product with my formula. I imported the products afterward. Crystal products gained a good market position, especially the hair gel, which gained a loyal customer base. Several years passed, and I had enough financial capability to have my own factory. But since the sales were good, I procrastinated. However, one Saturday at 11 AM on a hot summer day, I decided to have my own production unit, produce the final product there, and interact with the customers. I remember that day well. I had gone for a consultation at a company called Nosh Daru Farabi. We were in the meeting room. The doors and windows were open, and the crows were cawing outside. The pleasant aroma from the shampoo production section filled my nostrils. That day's meet-

ing was about the factory's lack of profitability because it was operating at only one-third of its production capacity.
When I talked to the factory manager about the final meeting, he thanked me for my collaboration and mentioned that he wanted to sell the factory. It was on that hot summer day at 11 AM that I made my decision. I asked, "Will you sell it to me?" He replied, "Yes, who better than you? How will you make the payments?"

The factory, spanning 4,200 square meters with a 1,200 square meter warehouse, was priced at 450 million tomans. After extensive negotiations, we agreed on a price of 440 million tomans, payable in 11 installments of 40 million tomans each. Fortune smiled upon me! Soon, the factory was mine. It was the perfect time to transfer the production of Crystal products to Iran and start local manufacturing.

I began negotiations with the French factory to obtain a licensing certificate. Since I had developed the formula myself and wasn't particularly dependent on the French factory, they agreed to issue the certificate for 5,000 euros. I received the certificate, which was also verified by the embassy and the Chamber of Commerce, and thus began the licensed production of Crystal.

As usual, business was thriving. A while later, we added the brand Rinozit to cater to different tastes. Around 2008, I met one of the industry's leaders. He suggested that we expand the business through a partnership. The sales were good, and there was potential for growth. His proposal tempted me, and we became 50-50 partners. This turned out to be one of the biggest mistakes of my career.

I was still young and inexperienced, unaware that a 50-50 partnership is not feasible. It might work for investments, but in decision-making, it's impractical because there always needs to be a final decision-maker.

Not long after our partnership, problems arose. My partner, who owned a tube manufacturing plant, sent 2 billion tubes to the company, but we failed to sell them within the stipulated time. Additionally, he had negotiated a property deal worth 1 billion tomans, which, due to our partnership issues, also required compensation. This left me 3 billion tomans in debt to him. He found a replacement for himself, took his 3 billion tomans, and sold his share. We were in a deadlock for several months, and I no longer wanted to continue the 50-50 arrangement. My reasoning was that, being much larger than me, they could significantly dilute my shares with a slight capital increase.

One day, I arrived to find both the factory and the warehouse sealed. I was helpless. Shortly after, we had a meeting where he suggested either I buy his share or he buys mine; otherwise, the factory and warehouse would remain sealed. Naturally, I preferred to retain the factory. We agreed to set a price.

Six billion tomans! He also stipulated that he would only accept checks from certain individuals he named. What was I to do?

I sought help from our sales representatives. I wrote a letter announcing the pre-sale of our products, slightly reducing the pre-sale prices. The purchases began. At that time, our products never stayed on the shelves and sold quickly. With the reduced prices, the sales pace increased even more. Within two weeks, I managed to gather the funds and repurchased the company. Everything returned to normal, and business was booming again. I had monthly sales of 15 billion tomans.

I reinvested the profits in various ventures. The company experienced exceptional growth until late 2012 and early 2013.

There's an old saying: "The fountain rises to a point, then it falls." In 2013, the dollar's value suddenly surged to 3,000 tomans. The market came to a standstill, and everything stagnated. Prices skyrocketed overnight. I had based all my plans on 15 billion tomans in monthly sales. My sales plummeted from 15 billion tomans a month to 4 billion. Projects were halted, checks bounced, and payments were delayed. Our assets lost two-thirds of their value overnight. In these plans, I had created about 40 billion tomans in obligations. I had prepared new brands and ordered new containers for the products, only to face this predicament. Those days of financial hardship were tough. Out of necessity, I turned to borrowing money at high interest rates, what we call "usury money," and borrowed 40 billion tomans to cover some payments and obligations.

From 2013 to late 2015, I repaid 60 billion tomans for the 40 billion I had borrowed and still had 170 billion tomans in debt. Sometimes I paid daily interest rates as high as 1%. Nothing can describe how I felt during those days. All I felt was that it shouldn't have turned out this way. I felt like I hadn't thought things through enough; that I wasn't good enough, and this destroys a person from within. Sometimes, because you can't escape the circumstances, you blame yourself. When I look back on those days, I realize that many of the issues were beyond my control. Everything had shut down. Sometimes, I wouldn't shave for weeks. I wanted everything to stop. I stopped watching TV, I didn't turn on the car radio, and I even lost the joy of talking. When I came home, I stayed in silence. I wouldn't finish my meals. Doubt and the feeling of having made mistakes consumed me. During those moments, I felt like there was nobody inside me. I was going through a long, dark night that seemed never-ending. I was completely worn out. One night, I sat alone without turning on the lights in my office. I opened the window, breathed in the cool morning air, and realized that continuing in this state was impossible. I didn't want to antagonize life or become its enemy. I couldn't remain in this hopeless and inactive state until one night I might die of a heart attack from the stress or die alone with my mouth open.

I realized that if I wanted to wake up every morning and continue my life, I couldn't let despair take over and drag me down. I accepted it! I accepted that this situation had happened for whatever reason, and now was not the time to sit and mourn it. I had known this feeling of loneliness and sorrow years ago when I was younger and had to barter my share, walking for hours with this dreadful and terrifying feeling.

I thought about it and realized that I loved my work, my history among the producers, importers, entering the factory, moving through the floors, examining documents, inspecting the production workshop, noting the rhythm of work, the smell of raw materials, watching the workers' faces, shaking hands with them, searching through the lists of materials, observing the production floor with my eyes and taking notes on the small details, not forgetting them, not forgetting anyone, holding the product bottles, going to the parking lot and greeting those who came to the factory for minor tasks whom I might never see again. I loved the smell of the production hall, I loved greeting and receiving reports from the workers. I couldn't let go of all these connections. Where was the problem? I needed to increase my financial knowledge. I needed to give more importance to financial matters. I had to bring everything out of thc back of my mind and operate scientifically and methodically. The fact that I could produce a product for 4,000 tomans and sell it for 16,000 tomans and still incur losses showed that something was wrong. Perhaps this was my best chance to realize that my weakness was my inability to read a financial statement, to analyze a financial report, but this weakness didn't mean I should abandon everything.

This was the life I had chosen and fought for, and I respected it, but I was exhausted. I was stuck in a grueling, exhausting game and didn't know how to get out of it. I told myself: "Either take control of your destiny and perform a miracle or bury your life. That's it. When you don't know something, don't run away from it; instead, dive into it, spend time on it. Take the courses. The worst thing you can do is ignore it."

The person who grabbed my collar that night of despair and pulled me out of that darkness was no one but myself.

The next morning, I dragged myself into the shower and, after a long time, shaved. I took out the last suit I had bought from the closet and wore it. When I looked at myself in the mirror, I saw the hollows under my eyes. I felt how much weight I had lost. I put on my best perfume, tidied my hair, grabbed my briefcase, and set off without my car. I walked part of the way and made my final decision. I went to court, declared bankruptcy, and requested a grace period to pay off my debts. However, there was no patience; many creditors filed lawsuits, and I spent six months in prison, then was released six months later with a confirmed bankruptcy ruling.

I sold everything. I sold the Farabi Elixir factory, my first factory, the Crystal brand with its production rights and all the products we had in the warehouses up to that point; the Rinozit brand with its product rights and all its productions, the house in Dubai, the mechanized dairy farm in Hashtgerd, and everything else I had acquired over the years. I was left with nothing and still had 110 billion tomans in debt out of 170 billion. I had paid off 60 billion tomans. I still had myself and my knowledge. I started production on a contract basis, and the only thing I kept was the second factory I had purchased.

The new brand had no name or recognition. Sales were challenging, although good products quickly find their place in the market, it still took time. Naturally, I had to organize the sales. Without sales, production has no meaning. I began searching and found a store called 40-50, which had become well-known and was doing well at the time. It was an online store with a dedicated customer base; they did good advertising and sold well. We entered negotiations, and by supplying part of the hygiene products, some of the debts were paid this way. Shortly after, the Badran marketing network emerged. This network of home-based and young marketers had just started and pre-paid for products. They had created a strong network of energetic and active young people. I talked to them, proposing that I supply the goods and they pay upon sale. With these excellent terms, they quickly agreed, and the products sold rapidly. I paid off about 20-30 billion tomans of debt this way.

I also worked with another small network company called Nafis Heritage. It was better than nothing but not very active. If I had to compare, while Badran had 10-12 billion in purchases, Nafis had only 100 million. However, they had very good and active marketers and employees.

Once I had some money in hand, the first thing I did was repurchase Crystal and Rinozit. Crystal was my identity, my brand,

and I was like a gardener who had nurtured this tree since it was a small seed; I couldn't hand it over to someone else. Fortunately, the new owners had not been able to make good, profitable use of the factory, and I bought it back cheaper than what I had sold it for.

In 2017, the Ministry of Industry issued regulations for marketing companies, stating that they could no longer sell foreign goods and that the goods they sold had to be their own production. These regulations made things very difficult for small companies. Nafis was on the brink of closure. The situation had changed, and it was possible to negotiate with them. I asked them what they planned to do next. They said there was nothing they could do since they were not producers. I offered to buy their license for 600 million tomans. I had thought about this before and considered all aspects. I wasn't going to act recklessly. This proposal was based on a real and well-planned strategy. They said they needed time to consider the offer, and I had time. I wasn't in a hurry to carry out this big task, and my patience eventually paid off; the deal was finalized for around 600 million tomans.

The next step was to find the right people for the job. Years of experience had taught me that if I wanted to start something strong, I had to start with strong people. Skilled and powerful individuals might demand higher salaries, but when you entrust them with a task, you can rest assured. These people have ideas. Over the years, working with marketing companies, I became acquainted with many of their powerful and high-ranking leaders. Most of them were dissatisfied due to delays in commission payments, untimely supply of goods, and incomplete deliveries. I invited those I knew to be capable individuals, and they all came willingly due to our previous acquaintance. I suggested they join Nafis under special conditions: they would only pay the company the profit from production, and I would have nothing to do with the sales commissions. This was an exceptional opportunity for everyone.

We launched in November 2017. The first month we made 100 million tomans, the second month 300 million, and the third month 700 million. The sales cycle picked up and grew rapidly, reaching a monthly sales figure of about 200 billion tomans five years later.

Today, we have reached a point where the small company that was on the verge of closing now employs 1,100 staff members and has 4,000 marketers, who on average receive commissions ranging from 6 million to 1 billion tomans. We now operate two large production plants, one in Salafchegan and another in Eshtehard, and have set up a capillary distribution network for pharmacies and galleries across Iran. Many talented, capable, and energetic young people collaborate with us. In addition to the two established brands, Crystal and Rhinosit, we have introduced new brands like Garni, Ward Color, and Romina, each with several sub-products.

Today, I am no longer financially at risk because I faced and addressed my managerial weaknesses. Whenever I encounter a shortcoming, I seek the expertise of knowledgeable individuals. Great people bring great successes with them. Currently, I have the warehouse manager from Digikala, a strong and capable individual, and a proficient financial manager who is well-versed in budgeting. If I make a mistake, he corrects it. I also have a doctor who cultivated the first medicinal mushroom, Ganoderma, in Iran. All these contributions have helped streamline our operations.

I have realized that even if one stumbles occasionally, they only fall a few steps down if the ground beneath them is firm. My firm ground was my knowledge. Once I resolved the minor and major issues, took off my shoes, and opened my eyes comfortably, I felt we needed products beyond the ordinary. I wanted to leverage my abilities to produce a unique, luxury product that people would talk about, negotiate over, and present proudly. This idea came to me on an autumn afternoon.

During a trip, while hiking a gentle slope in a pristine forest, I stopped to catch my breath. Standing with my back to the slope, I inhaled deeply. It had rained the night before; the air was fresh, and the ground was slippery. Although the sun was weak, the sky was still cloudy. I sat down, looked around, and saw no one. There was complete silence, as if everything was waiting for an event. The forest extended up the mountain, and the smell of rain-soaked earth and small chamomile flowers filled my senses. An unusual calm washed over me. Suddenly, the thought struck me: I wanted a product that embodied excitement, tranquility, depth, and nostalgia.

Upon returning to Tehran, I started working on new products based on aromatherapy. Aromatherapy, in a word, is scent therapy, using familiar smells to evoke distant memories or feelings of happiness and joy, promoting the health and well-being of the body, mind, and spirit. Scents are powerful reminders.

Based on this, a series of interconnected products was created. These included diffusers, scented spritzers, body oils, creams, or lotions for massage or topical use, facial steamers, shampoos, hair conditioners, moisturizing creams, air fresheners with familiar scents like cinnamon, vanilla, lemon, rose, jasmine, sage, eucalyptus, ginger, lavender, peppermint, and rosemary. These nostalgic scents have a profound effect on the nerves.

Afterward, a more specialized and premium product line was developed: Blackberry products formulated based on stem cells, including anti-spot and anti-hair loss solutions. These products were specifically designed for our network marketing because they have a strong selling point. Clearly, these specialized products cannot be offered in pharmacies due to their relatively high price and the lack of time for sellers to explain them thoroughly, which in 90% of cases, potential customers would ignore.

In network marketing, we rely heavily on our close connections and their support. You start by introducing your product to close friends, family, and neighbors. They are willing to take the time to listen to you. Success in this field depends on engaging in discussions and negotiations, and attracting new customers through these interactions. Therefore, we needed a product that our marketers could proudly and confidently discuss and promote. For example, there's not much to say about a regular shampoo, but when discussing a unique cream, questions arise: What are stem cells? Why should it contain gold? These questions create marketing opportunities.

Initially, I sell a cream that contains stem cells and 24-carat gold, promising to smooth out wrinkles. If this pitch leads to a sale, the next step is to encourage that person to join my network to receive discounts. Once they join, the third step is to persuade them to recruit others: not only will they get discounts, but they will also earn commissions if someone they recruit makes a purchase.

An interesting story that led to a significant development arose from a problem. Items purchased online were being shipped to customers via postal services. One evening, I was alone in the office reviewing reports when the phone rang. I ignored it at first, thinking the caller could try again later or speak to the staff in the morning. The phone kept ringing persistently. Finally, I decided to answer it.

As soon as I said "hello," an angry woman on the other end started without a greeting: "I ordered a beauty pack for my friend's birthday last week. It was supposed to arrive in two days, but it's been a week, and it just arrived in terrible condition. When I complained to the postal worker, he rudely told me to contact the post office or return the package if I was so upset." She expressed her frustration about the poor packaging and customer service and then hung up abruptly.

At first, I was taken aback, but then I understood her frustration. After all, we went through great lengths to ensure our products reached customers satisfactorily. If customers were unhappy, all our efforts were in vain. We were the second-largest customer of the postal service after Digikala, shipping around 200,000 packages a month. Even if only 1% of customers were dissatisfied, that was a significant number.

This led me to consider creating a dedicated postal service for delivering our products. After consulting and planning, Nafis Express was born. We worked hard to address previous issues, ensuring packages were delivered quickly, intact, and respectfully. Now, we cover 24 to 48 hours in Tehran and 72 hours in other cities, and we are looking to offer our services to other online stores as well.

Today, we are launching a new perfume and cologne production line in a 6,000-square-meter factory in the Salafchegan Free Trade Zone to facilitate the import of specialized containers.

We have also established the Shavaz website, a sales platform that offers both our products and those from other brands.

Our next plan is to add a production unit for dietary supplements. To stay competitive, we constantly innovate and update our strategies to match market preferences. Looking back, I am happy. I am content with myself and even grateful for all the challenges and obstacles we faced. Every disappointment, doubt, exhaustion, and time away from my family was an integral part of the journey. In times of calm, there is so much to see and learn in this world, countless paths to explore. Every valuable achievement in life comes after overcoming its related negative experiences. Attempts to escape, evade, or suppress these experiences only make the repercussions more severe. Life is full of inevitable struggles and challenges that cannot be avoided. Mistakes and problems are part of the beauty of being human.

These years of triumphs and setbacks have taught me that the most crucial thing in life is not to care about everything. Indifference yields the best results. This does not mean being apathetic towards your goals. Unlike many young people today who unfortunately don't care about anything, it means prioritizing your focus. Once you choose a goal and path, disregard the other distractions. Ignore the hardships, criticism, failures, and financial difficulties. If you care about everything, you will waste your energy on trivial matters. If you worry about a scratch on your car, traffic, a colleague not greeting you, yesterday's weak tea, a dead remote battery, a burnt-out kitchen light, or delayed text messages, you will exhaust your energy and have nothing left for more important issues. Imagine you have a limited number of cares each day—say, ten. Where and how will you spend them? Your presence will be significant in some areas but less so in others. Therefore, it's crucial to identify what truly matters.

A successful life is not one where you care about everything; instead, it's about having a few important things that truly matter. My advice to young people is to get to know themselves and their talents, then disregard the rest and follow their path. If they can identify their strengths and invest in them, they will certainly succeed. Perhaps someone doesn't have the physical ability to become a professional athlete, but they might excel as a salesperson. The key is to find that talent and pursue it with passion. The universe rewards enthusiasm but first tests its authenticity. It throws challenges in your path, and if you overcome them without retreating, you earn your reward. Unlike us, the universe knows the value of its priorities and doesn't waste them easily.

We lack nothing in this country. In terms of knowledge, technology, and production, I can confidently say we are at a high level. If our products and those from international brands like L'Oréal were presented in unbranded packaging, they would be of equal quality. However, we are weak in international packaging and marketing. These are areas where young people, though not easily, can invest and study, as there is plenty of room for growth. But wasting time on the internet certainly won't bring a bright future for anyone.

Analyzing the Success Factors of

the Founder of Nafis Holdings and Brands Like Crystal, Renozit, Garnie, and Others

Years ago, scientists conducted an intriguing experiment. They placed two mice in water where the likelihood of drowning was high. After a few minutes, they took the mice out. Once the mice had dried and caught their breath, they were put back into the water. This time, the mice swam and struggled for nearly fifty hours to survive. In the previous experiment, these mice had only managed to stay afloat for about twenty to thirty minutes before drowning. But why was there such a difference? Why did the mice, with their unique nervous systems and behaviors, manage to endure so much longer the second time?

The Power of Hope

Scientist's attribute this to the power of hope. In the second experiment, the mice were hopeful that someone would save them, unlike in the first experiment where they had no such hope.

When the mice had no hope, they quickly gave up and perished. Hope is something that occurs in the mind and somehow generates mental resilience. This mental resilience and the ability to not give up are key factors that give us the strength to keep going. As you can see, success happens first in the mind before it manifests in reality and sets real-world forces in motion.

Where Does Hope Come From?

Have you ever wondered where the power of hope comes from and how this flowing spring is nourished? One of the streams that feed this reservoir is the literature of personal development or individual success. Here, realities enter the mind and carve out specific neural pathways. These realities create the foundations of mental faith and certainty. The belief that success is not merely the result of luck, fate, or destiny, but rather the outcome of planning, feedback, persistent effort, and not giving up. Until the last century, such concepts were seldom discussed. People thought our actions and behaviors were influenced by external forces like society, family, genetics, and history, implying a deterministic outlook on life. However, experiences emerged that challenged this deterministic view. As the frequency and volume of these experiences increased, a group of thinkers realized that this was possible and repeatable. Repetition, the essence of science, means uncovering rules and formulas that can be systematic and replicable. Thus, within the science of psychology, fields like personal development psychology, success psychology, and positive psychology were born, eventually evolving into disciplines that are understandable and usable by the general public.

From Science to Faith, and from Faith to Hope

The truth is that the science and knowledge of success create faith and certainty in the mind. This faith can lead to the generation of hope, which fosters mental resilience. This mental resilience prevents us from giving up and allows us to endure longer even in the physical world. In the external world, visible and tangible successes belong to those who persist, resist fatigue, and keep pursuing their goals. The power of hope is the most constructive force for instilling mental resilience and indomitability in individuals. Until recently, people did not fully grasp the power of hope and thought that everything happened by itself, unrelated to their actions. In such cases, there was no hope, and like the mice in the initial experiment, failure occurred swiftly. However, when you see people achieving remarkable success through planning, effort, feedback, and adjusting their approaches, hope arises within you. This hope leads to behavioral resilience, which in turn leads to success. This encapsulates the essence of personal development literature and success generation.

Revisiting the Lives of the Successful

One of the major occurrences in this context is revisiting the lived experiences of successful individuals. This means analyzing the experiences of people who have come forward and succeeded. These books and biographies create faith and certainty in your mind, leading to the generation of ample hope. This abundant hope fosters behavioral and strategic resilience, culminating in success. The examination of the lives of individuals like Peyman Kianian is relevant and noteworthy in this regard. These individuals teach us how to start, how to continue, and how to reach our goals. Collecting such insights can contribute to the science of individual success and strengthen the power of hope in our minds.

Chapter One

In revisiting the life of Peyman Kianian, the first question that might arise is: Why does someone start from zero and achieve such success, even after experiencing terrifying failures, and still manage to embrace success? As mentioned in the introduction, part of this approach ties back to the literature on personal development and the principles of success. But how is such an occurrence explained and justified in the context of personal development literature?

A Constructive Formula

Jack Canfield, in his insightful book "The Success Principles," highlights an interesting point that revolves around taking full responsibility for one's life. He states that you can only achieve great success if you decide to take full responsibility for your results and behaviors. If you only take partial responsibility for your actions and outcomes, you will not put in the necessary effort. Canfield mentions a rule he learned from a psychologist friend that always helps him achieve outstanding results by taking full responsibility. But what is this rule and how does it apply?

The formula he refers to is: Success = Event + Your Response

You've probably heard this principle before. It's often said that many events in life happen beyond our control. So, how does personal willpower and success find justification in this context? To reach our desired conclusion, we must consider a few key assumptions:

1. First Point: Many events in life occur outside our control, but our reaction to these events is entirely within our power to define and manage. We certainly have complete control over our reactions to these events and occurrences.
2. Second Point: Even if we have limited control over our reactions and feedback to events, we at least have full control over how we think about them. Just like Viktor Frankl in the Nazi death camps; despite everything being taken from him, he still had the power of his thoughts and perspectives, which gave him significant freedom to gradually build upon.
3. Third Point: By considering the first two points, you can make your future more predictable. From today onward, you are creating events and circumstances that will produce a more desirable situation for you in the future, practically leading you to success. This doesn't mean that unpredictable events won't occur; it means you are making some of these future unpredictable events more manageable.

From these points, we can conclude that we humans possess significant power, autonomy, and willpower to make necessary changes in our surrounding world. Understanding and acknowledging these points lead to action because you can't act on what you don't know.

The Circle of Influence and Circle of Concern

Dr. Stephen Covey, in his book "The 7 Habits of Highly Effective People," explains this concept well. He discusses two circles that are nested within each other. The larger circle encompasses all the activities we can engage in and all the events that happen in our lives. This circle includes both the things we have control over and the things we do not.

Within this larger circle, draw a smaller circle centered around the middle. This smaller circle represents areas where you can have influence—where you have power or can gain power to manage events. These events fall into categories of direct influence, indirect influence, and non-influence. In the first case, you engage directly. In the second, you manage outcomes by influencing others. For events beyond your control, you manage your mindset and perspective. Altogether, these represent the areas where you can take action.

Gradually, these events increase, enlarging your circle of influence. The larger this circle grows, the more success you experience. Some people strive to make their circle of influence as large as their circle of concern, and these individuals tend to be extraordinarily successful.

Success Breeds Success

There's a well-known Persian proverb that says, "Money brings money." Some people also link this principle to the law of attraction, suggesting that like attracts like. Consequently, if you want to achieve more success, you should start with small successes. These small successes will gradually trigger other successes in a pendulum effect, leading to increasing achievements. Initial successes act like a snowball rolling downhill, collecting more snow and growing larger and larger, eventually becoming unstoppable. This snowball only picks up related particles like snow, not dirt or stones. Similarly, in the context of "success breeds success," even if you have little control in your life, starting with small successes can attract larger ones. It's that simple.

A Known Secret

This phenomenon isn't new; people have operationalized it for many years. They start with small tasks, and with each success, their confidence grows. Increased confidence leads to attempting slightly bigger tasks. Each successful task results in even greater confidence, creating a cycle of growth. The more tasks they undertake, the faster the cycle turns, leading to more significant success. This pattern is evident in the lives of people like Peyman Kianian. They began with smaller tasks, and with each success, their confidence increased. They quickly understood the secret of this cycle of personal development and progress, utilizing it to achieve more success. Each additional success brought them one step closer to their ultimate goal. What more could a success-seeker desire?

Chapter Two

As mentioned in the introduction, the greatest mental attribute that empowers us to continue is hope. The hope that things will lead to the desired outcomes if they follow certain principles. This optimism prompts our minds to work and move forward. Therefore, the most debilitating mental illnesses are those that impact a person's willpower. Willpower stems from the mind, and when the mind is sick, no willpower is generated. Without willpower, no current situation will transform into a desirable one; it's as simple as that.

Is Social Status Immutable?

One of the most encouraging aspects of personal development and success is realizing that even if you are born into a poor and low-status family, there is a strong possibility that with perseverance, you can achieve great things. This perspective was not always common; people used to believe that social and familial status was somcthing unchangeable, and that we would remain within the same social and cultural status into which we were born. But is this really the case?

Standard, efficiency matters, not family or lineage.

In recent decades, however, this thinking has been proven wrong time and again. This is because fundamentally the standards have changed. They have tried to define standards around efficiency and final output rather than other things. When such a standard is considered, it is natural that social and familial shifts happen more easily; because anyone can achieve such successes, and these successes define and clarify individuals' subsequent positions. Brian Tracy has repeatedly emphasized in his educational books on wealth creation and success that the number of self-made millionaires in the world today and in America is unprecedented compared to any period in history. He defines self-made millionaires as those who started from scratch and built all their wealth themselves; meaning such fortunes did not come through inheritance, legacy, proximity to powerful individuals, luck, or winning specific competitions.

Wealth is important, but...

You might wonder why we emphasize success so much in the context of wealth creation. There are several reasons for this. Firstly, in today's world, wealth and economics are the determinants of global power. Therefore, everyone strives to demonstrate themselves in the realm of economics and wealth creation to make progress. The next point is, as Jim Rohn puts it, the first million dollars is important to earn because the subsequent millions can easily follow. But more importantly, it is the person you become in pursuit of this amount, whether it's the first million dollars or, as we Iranians say, the first billion tomans, that matters. You have become more resourceful, sharper, more strategic, enhanced your mental faculties, and cultivated dozens of other habits within yourself. Essentially, without these mental and practical habits, wealth cannot be accumulated, because we know wealth and other successes are not pursued but attracted. Wealth remains like a butterfly; if you chase it, it will elude you, but if you have a flower, it will come and sit on your shoulder without trouble. Therefore, you must cultivate habits within yourself to attract this wealth, otherwise it will not happen for you. On the other hand, we know that character is defined by the habits we possess. So when you have such good habits, you have transformed into a good character. In fact, in this context, self-improvement is more important than the ultimate goal of acquiring wealth. Isn't this motivating?

The rules of our time

Thus, our rule is as follows: you live in an era where efficiency, power in wealth creation, and your creativity are predominantly focused. If you instill these qualities in yourself, as a result, you can experience good social and economic mobility; meaning you can move to a better neighborhood, have better facilities, enroll your children in better schools, go on better trips, and so on. These naturally contribute to the growth of your social and familial status; because your family members, including your children and descendants, start from a better point and strive. Ultimately, the spark of hope that ignites in your mind, giving you the necessary motivation, is far more important than this social and class transformation itself.

Forces needed for success

These are the energies and powers that ensure eternal success and never cease. Fundamentally, wealth, economic power, factories, production lines, machinery, assets, etc., are merely natural consequences; you don't even need to think about them. Let's clarify the eternal force of success with an example. When you work well and dedicate a lot of perseverance and energy to your work, you may get tired, but you feel good. This is something many overlooks; that the effort for success fundamentally creates a mental state in you, where the main goal itself is striving for success. Isn't that so? Conversely, when you lack perseverance and constantly complain, lacking the patience, heart, and mind for effort, your mental state deteriorates and may even create significant psychological problems for you. These two examples we mentioned show that one of the most important reasons and goals for striving for success is having a good and extraordinary mindset that it grants you. With this mindset, anything can be accomplished. Note that even if this effort for success doesn't bring anything tangible for you and only brings you this good and excellent mindset, it in itself is a great success. What more do you want from success, wealth, and high social status? Enjoy your good and happy present. Now, alongside this main goal, surely wealth, good income, and other apparent successes will also come your way, which practically result from the same perspective we mentioned. They say that focusing on money can turn you and your life into a cold, dry, and soulless existence; because fundamentally wealth and money are soulless things and only gain importance because they allow you to have better opportunities in life. With these points in mind, your focus should be on having a good mindset rather than simply acquiring wealth. Wealth itself will come and attract you.

The magnificent power of hope

All these things we mentioned are the result of that hope and winning mentality that was mentioned. Hope allows you to understand that you can start from zero and reach where you want. You just need to expend the necessary energy and perseverance and not give up; have mental and emotional resilience.

Chapter Three

When we review the life of Peyman Kianian, we encounter the concept of network marketing more prominently. One of the reasons for his success, even when he faced severe setbacks and spent several mornings in prison due to his debts, must be attributed to his familiarity with network marketing. Here, we need to delve a bit more into traditional sales systems versus modern sales systems to understand what we are talking about.

Traditional Sales vs. Modern Sales

In traditional commerce systems, sales happen through the producer. That is, a producer tries to transfer their goods and services to their own agents. These agents then attempt to deliver these goods and services to retail points or what are commonly known as banks and purchasing and selling channels. They also endeavor to transfer these goods and services to end consumers. The final goods and services do not retain the exact price that the initial producer had in mind. Why? Because in this process, the costs of transferring to agents and retail points, as well as the profits these individuals and systems earn, need to be added to the product or service. Now, in modern commerce, a system called network marketing has been established, the philosophy of which is to eliminate intermediaries and directly transfer goods and services to consumers. Here, you as a consumer are directly connected to the producer and can even participate in the process of transferring products and services to others, potentially earning profits in the process. This means that as a consumer, you receive goods and services at a lower price than the market rate and can also allocate a portion of the profit to yourself if you transfer them to others.

Boundless Successes

One of the interesting points about this system of distributing goods and services is that there are no boundaries to your successes, unlike in the traditional system where you face many limitations. As a traditional banker, how much can you stock in your warehouses and how much can you transfer to large and small customers? However, in a more modern and contemporary system like network marketing, you have no limits to providing goods and services. This is why some merchants have introduced this system as the future of world commerce, despite all the difficulties and misuses that have occurred along the way!

The Thrill of Borderless Success

Network marketing has been so thrilling for some groups that they have conducted extensive research, written books, and produced content about it. One such person is Mark Yarnell, who wrote the famous book "Your First Year in Network Marketing," which has been well received. In his book, according to Webster's authoritative dictionary, he defines longevity as staying alive, especially after the death of others: "Longevity means surviving when others have left the business and is the beginning of wealth creation." He also considers doubting oneself to be exhausting and disheartening: "Nothing can undermine your behavior and speech like doubt. Nothing can empty your emotional fuel tank like doubt." Interestingly, he contrasts the negative view on this matter by stating, "Take pride in your profession. Be happy that thousands of people can achieve their dreams through you. Be a strong advocate for your job." He points out that professionals in this field are more interested in achieving higher amounts in checks for their performance rather than higher positions, travel rewards, and vacations, which motivates them and sets them apart from others: "Focus on getting higher amount checks, not higher positions. In this profession, wealthy employees are only excited about high value checks. The poorer ones just travel and win signs. Focus on the legitimacy of buying wealth for yourself." Finally, he mentions that the more you share in this profession, the more wealth and success you will achieve and that the only secret to success is sustainability; means when others are small, you can still continue.

The Teachings of Jim Rohn the Great

One of the other famous books published in this area is by Jim Rohn. You know Jim Rohn? In the United States, he is known as a business philosopher and has been a professor for reputable people such as Anthony Robbins and Brian Tracy. He wrote the magic part-time book on this subject, which has many bright points. Now let's read more about this industry while reading a book about Peyman Kianian and reading about Network Marketing, read more about this industry from a person like Jim Rohn.

I realized in my early youth and adolescence that I could make money for work. This was interesting to me, but I understood that this way you could make money, but you couldn't make a lot of money;

Until I became familiar with network marketing. This work allowed me to make good income with part-time work. This system fundamentally changed my life and forever. That's why most of my life spent talking to others about it because it has a very efficient philosophy;

One of my greatest mental philosophies is that profiting is better than paying. You get paid for working and spending time, and it's just for living and debt to time;

My experience in network marketing has led me to acquire

specific skills. The first skill I learned was sales. This skill has brought about a tremendous change in my life. Selling was surprisingly straightforward; all you had to do was introduce your product, that's it.

Sales means sharing information, that's it.

In business, "sharing information" holds significant importance. You only talk to the customer about a product you have used yourself and the positive feedback from those who have benefited from it.

When I learned sales, my income increased fivefold. It laid the foundation for a professional life.

My first goal was to match the income from my full-time job with the earnings from my part-time work. This phenomenon is called the magic of part-time work. Just dedicating 10 to 15 hours a week is enough. If you do your job well, learn some skills and techniques, it won't take long for your part-time income (for becoming wealthy) to match your full-time job income. For me, this happened in less than six months. My second goal was to earn twice as much money with part-time work for wealth creation compared to my full-time job. After achieving this, I quit my full-time job and focused entirely on becoming wealthy. Let part-time work, do its magic for you. It doesn't take a lot of income to change your lifestyle; just an extra thousand dollars a month is enough. That's why part-time work is truly valuable because it can change anyone's way and style of life. This is also the key in network marketing to attract customers. Someone asks me, "How did you go on vacation three times this year? How did you buy two new cars, one for yourself and one for your spouse?" And I say, "Just with an extra thousand dollars a month." I suggest to them to start part-time work too. Note that if these thousand dollars came from a full-time job, no one would listen to your story. It's not necessarily money that changes your life, but how you use your money that transforms your life and changes your lifestyle. This, in turn, becomes a classic invitation in network marketing. Because people ask what you're doing. In addition, you can also invite others to your part-time job with these sentences. Say I have found a part-time job to create wealth that earns me as much as my full-time job. Would you like to hear my story? This story is really interesting.

The excitement is endless.

Now you understand the difference between modern and traditional commerce. Basically, the differences go back to philosophies, and in the end, it's in the real world that you see these differences. Until you know the work philosophy, no matter how far you go, you won't get anywhere and ultimately, you'll lose motivation. These are the same points that Peyman Kianian refers to. Like when you start "presenting" your customers, basically from the time the customer comes and doesn't always give you the "presentation" time, you will have a better time. You have time and can convince the other party and this will make you feel good. In the next moments you can even follow up on the exclusive presentation of products that may not exist outside the network and this will give you the unique feature. The next point is that when you try harder, you will get more. He mentions that he works with a network of tens of thousands of vendors who sometimes have a commission of up to two billion Tomans a month! Note that this is a commission and not a sale. In sales, you have to subtract the final price of the product from the final price of the sale to reach income and then profit. while the commission is just pure profit. Means that this person may have had ten times this amount. In which other business can such excitement exist?

Chapter Four

The key to success has clear rules that, if followed correctly, can take you to its peaks. One of these rules is perseverance and of course direction. Another rule is to continue to move and try; means that while you have to try hard, your effort must be such that, as Darren Hardy says, you are supposed to have a lifelong job. Of course, in all your life you cannot work eight hours a day and read and after a while you will get tired. But at one, two hours of study and concentrated efforts, it can always be operational. According to the compound effect law, this continuity after a while will lead to differences and shining results. The rule of distinction in "direction" is another key rule that, along with the rules of success, we have already mentioned. Means that at the beginning of the matter you have to decide where you want to go and then choose a path that leads to such results.

For example, if you want to become the CEO of a government company, you must follow a path and if you want to become a self-made millionaire, your path must be different. It is natural that moving in a different direction will waste your success and will make you, after a while, get where you want to go. Becoming an entrepreneur is also an idea that must be specified and understood direction and steps are taken. Otherwise, if there is, no matter how hard you work and get more feedback and build more social networks and ... again, you will not get to the point you need. In fact, it can be said that this direction is one of the most important reasons for success; because if not understood well, you are actually moving away from your main goal, just as easily. Money-making routes the truth is that to become an entrepreneur or a self-made millionaire, you may need to discover and understand your own direction and take a step in it. For Brian Tracy, in his wealth education books, he knows people who are engaged in the field in four categories: 1. Employees and those who work for others in exchange for wages; 2. Self-employed who have made a profession and earn money by providing services through their expertise; 3. Those who have created a business and make money through production and so on; 4. Those who have money and capital and instead of working as employees or working for themselves or having a business, prefer to invest this money and benefit from its talents. He says that to create wealth, naturally, everyone in any of these four houses that are present can take action; but the statistics say that most wealth creators are people who have created a business or made various investments in various places and have benefited from its talents. Although a worker or a self-employed person can work hard and collect money and start a business after a while or invest. Or, according to Brian Tracy, in the same field, in the employee or self-employed sector, they receive good rewards and practically come to the ranks of millionaires. But the point here is that the abundance of these groups is low; just as the abundance of those who make wealth by means of music and art and acting and sports and... is compared to those who have businesses and businesses. Established or invested, it is still far less intense.

It seems like the text you provided is a reflection on the journey and philosophy of Payman Kianian, emphasizing the importance of setting goals and having a purpose-driven life. Here's a summary and paraphrasing of the text:

Payman Kianian's life story illustrates a significant change in direction. From humble beginnings, he excelled academically and was encouraged by professors to teach and even grade others' work while still a student. His diligence as an employee earned him a reputation as someone everyone wanted to have on their team. Through specialization and effective work in various businesses, he accumulated considerable wealth. However, he harbored a desire to create his own business and be his own boss.

So, what did he do? He changed direction. When his employers realized he wanted to change course, some were even willing to offer him higher income. Some were willing to become partners with him as well. He still decided to establish his own business and went after a new direction that would allow him to reach his goals more comfortably.

This path wasn't easy, and he experienced setbacks and even betrayal from his partner. But he persevered, paying the price he felt was necessary. Along the way, he used network marketing and injected his ideas, paying off his debts and achieving a very good economic position. All these were the result of two things: Understanding what he needed to do or was interested in doing and where he wanted to go.

Deciding what path and direction would take him to his destination.

Putting his foot in this way and moving forward, knowing that the farther he went, the closer he would get to his goal.

Chapter Five

In Chapter Five, Payman Kianian discusses the interesting point of the aimlessness of the new generation. He believes strongly that today's youth are severely indulged and do not understand goals; they are heavily aimless. Their lives are aimless, constantly pursuing short-term benefits and pleasures, which is somewhat called the murderer of long-term successes. Payman Kianian is strongly goal-oriented and enjoys having an annual goal-setting notebook and achieving it. The tick he uses to get to his goals is enjoyable for him. Goals are strongly influential in success. According to Brian Tracy, "Goals are the fuel in the furnace of achievement." Payman Kianian refers to a liner that in the event you

The Big Difference

This is the big difference that many might not notice. He believes that simply producing a product and seeing it on the shelves of pharmacies and large stores is the ultimate pleasure for him—a sentiment that many might not grasp and dismiss as madness. However, entrepreneurs, in Steve Jobs' words, are the crazy ones who believe they can have goals that change the world; and indeed, they go ahead and change the world. They pay the price of this world-changing effort with their lives. But so, what? Time will pass, children will grow up, and... So, it's better to have achieved our goals and have had selflessness so that this time has passed, rather than just regret why we haven't achieved such things?

Chapter Six

The Impactful Difference

A lot can be said about the concept of selflessness. This concept defines whether our goals and actions lead to ultimate success or not. A very important point about this is that most citizens wonder if there really is a need to feel selfless? This crucial question determines what answers we should have for this purpose. You might be familiar with Grant Cardone. He has written extraordinary books in the field of success in business and personal life. Interestingly, his life situation was very tragic at first, and he had even consumed drugs to the extent that he had no hope of surviving. But when he passed this danger to health, he entered a new phase of his life. He succeeded in making hundreds of millions of dollars for himself and, according to him, permanently securing his family; because that's what he was so afraid of, and his mother was always worried, and even worried about buying food and clothes for her children.

Last Chapter

One of the interesting points that Cardone refers to is that you are not supposed to live your time alive, just work hard; But you also have to work for something as your own legacy. He talks about what your legacy really is; Money? wealth? A home? Physical and physical possessions? He thinks beyond these; That you pass on to future generations, who have started from scratch and achieved such success with your ideas, and they use your ideas and make their lives successful. Isn't that an extraordinary legacy? So, we shouldn't always have such a view that now we are seventy, eighty years old and why do we want all this wealth? the response is in inheritance; Legacy that we leave behind for our children and other citizens.

Unwavering perseverance

One of the constructive points that Kianian refers to is relentless perseverance. Whether working for others, attending university classes, or afterward, he deeply believed in perseverance and viewed himself as the epitome of this principle. He mentions that during his university studies, he once stayed awake for 72 hours straight to study his lessons and achieve the desired goal he had in mind. It's not without reason that Steve Jobs, the founder of Apple, noted that half of what sets entrepreneurs apart is sheer perseverance. But where does this sheer perseverance come from? Otherwise, everyone would want to have it, but few crack the code so quickly.

Enthusiasm and Purpose

Darren Hardy, in his influential book "The Compound Effect," dedicates an exceptional chapter to the power of purpose. He begins by acknowledging the value of willpower, but asserts that it alone is not sufficient. So, what's required? He suggests that what propels you into action and also ignites your willpower is the power of purpose—what we commonly refer to as motivation. Certainly, you understand better than I do that motivation signifies the collective force of an individual's purposes in various behaviors. When you possess a clear and powerful reason for doing something, you effortlessly pursue it without hesitation. Peyman Kianian also touches upon this point. He asserts that having a clear goal initially sparks motivation within you, and this motivation and enthusiasm automatically cultivate a strong willpower. This enables you to wake up easily in the mornings and charge towards your goals. He himself mentions that even during moments of failure, he woke up eagerly every morning and hurried towards his work and life. According to him, a suitable goal creates fervent enthusiasm, and fervent enthusiasm naturally awakens the willpower and discipline necessary to achieve that goal. This is why younger individuals must have good goals; without them, there will be no motivation and consequently no willpower, resulting in a generation facing idleness.

No Comparison

It's true that you must have perseverance and reach your goals, but this doesn't mean you should compare yourself today with others who may have started earlier, faced greater pressures, and experienced various failures. Such comparisons lead you to quickly conclude that you are lacking, while remaining unaware of the hardships the person you're comparing yourself to has endured. This itself becomes a catalyst for movement in you. Therefore, you must disregard comparisons.

Strengthening Weak Points

We all detest certain things, and these often become our weaknesses. Typically, where we fear, we appear weak, and this aversion is the reason behind it. Peyman Kianian mentions that one of the things he strongly disliked, a dislike that continued until five years ago, was financial matters. Interestingly, until five years ago, he rarely dealt with financial matters and, as he put it, mentally calculated everything. The reason for his failures was this; he lost money against his calculations. Later, he concluded that he should find expertise in financial matters. Even today, he recommends that entrepreneurs and creators must consider financial and accounting knowledge; they should not embark on this journey until they learn it; balance sheet reading and budgeting, for example. Maybe they hate these things, but, in any case, to be successful, they must do these things.

Human resources are decisive

Henry Ford, the founder of the Ford Motor Company, had an interesting idea in his time. He believed that the company should attract more specialized people and give them two or three times more wages than other companies. But why? Because they transferred a lifetime of expertise and experience to his company, and the profit he received in this way was much higher. Of course, he believed that in this way, other companies would deprive themselves of the presence of such valuable forces, which was somehow beneficial to them, although his main idea was to use their expertise. He said that instead of wanting to educate all his forces and take all expert advice, he attracted those forces to put more effort into their expertise, and that's why they're all useful.

Wealth Creation Skills

One intriguing point related to Peyman Kianian is that he sold one of his brands during a period when the exchange rate was 3,500 tomans per dollar, for 40 billion tomans. Five years later, he repurchased the same brand in a period where the exchange rate had risen to 30,000 tomans per dollar, for 20 billion tomans. If you calculate for inflation, he effectively repurchased the company at a twentieth of the original selling price! This demonstrates that those who bought the brand initially, expecting substantial profits, lacked the skills in management and wealth creation needed for such ventures. Therefore, it becomes evident that wealth and capital alone are not everything, and one must possess the necessary skills for success.

If you have the required skills and mindset, you can easily extract more profit and benefit from the smallest capital investments. So rather than focusing on the size of your wallet when starting a business, focus on the size of your mind and intellect. It's not without reason that Jim Rohn said, "Capital isn't that important in business. It's not money that brings you future, but your skills that do. If you have money and you don't have enough skills, you're still poor. If you have money but no desire for progress, it's uncertain where you're headed. If you have money but lack courage, you're a complete bankrupt. What we all need is little money and great courage. I work for people and when I look back, I see that money has never been important to me and I was just trying to attract people. What mattered to me was the initiative, desire, and effort of people."

The Attacker Mindset

In his prime, Michael Jordan once said: "Realizing that life provides the best things to the attacker's mind and to achieve this, one must go out and attack his goals and tasks and will not get anywhere by sitting inside home and having an inactive mindset." The reality is that successful individuals must have an aggressive mindset. This is a point that this entrepreneur also points out; that today's generation lacks such a mindset and is highly lazy and expects everything to come to them. He also mentions that perhaps we, as parents, have somehow been the cause and creator of such a mindset; because we have given our children everything they wanted. In the end, as Jim Rohn said, life responds to worthiness and dignity, not to need. So, act like life. Go out and sow the seeds of success as much as you can; to see the result of it. Doing nothing and waiting won't get you anywhere.

Iranian Great Entrepreneur Books are originally created by *Great Entrepreneur Institution* in Iran and you can access their books in Iran through this here:

www.karafarinanebozorg.com

Also, to access books all around the world click bellow:

www.kidsocado.com/greatentrepreneur

How to access kidsocado Publishing House

www.kidsocado.com/shop

www.ingramcontent.com/pod-product-compliance
Lightning Source LLC
Chambersburg PA
CBHW052151070526
44585CB00017B/2065

* 9 7 8 1 7 7 8 9 2 1 8 9 6 *